Terrific Trees

Written by Sarah Rice

Collins

Are trees terrific? From little shoots to towering trunks with colossal **crowns**, all trees are interesting!

Elderflower trees have short trunks and brown bark. The flowers have a strong smell.

Elderflowers can become soft drinks and jam.

Coastal redwood trees are the highest trees on the planet.

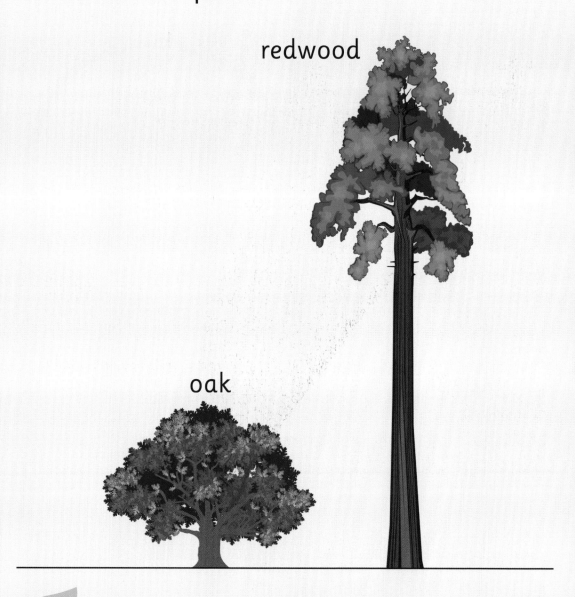

redwood

oak

If you stand at the bottom of the trunk the crown is hidden!

Redwood trees are **evergreen**.

Majestic kapok trees **inhabit tropical** rainforests like the Amazon.

They have sharp thorns and the flowers **emit** a smell that attracts bats.

Kapok seed pods contain silk cotton.

Banyan trees have adapted to cloak trees with strong roots.

They are parasitic, prospering by strangling the main tree.

The sap from rubber trees looks like milk and contains rubber.

Products such as car parts and boots consist of rubber.

Look out for a terrific tree near you!

Trees

Glossary

crowns: the top parts of trees

emit: to let out

evergreen: a tree that is never brown

inhabit: to exist in

tropical: a hot, wet setting

☙ After reading ☙

Letters and Sounds: Phase 4

Word count: 140

Focus on adjacent consonants with long vowel phonemes, e.g./t/ /r/ /ee/

Common exception words: of, to, the, all, by, are, you, they, have, like, come (become), little, out

Curriculum links: Science: Plants

National Curriculum learning objectives: Spoken language: ask relevant questions to extend their understanding and knowledge; Reading/word reading: read accurately by blending sounds in unfamiliar words containing GPCs that have been taught; Reading/comprehension: draw on what they already know or on background information and vocabulary provided by the teacher

Developing fluency

- Your child may enjoy hearing you read the book.
- You may wish to read the book together, with you reading the main text on each page and your child reading the captions in the tree trunks.

Phonic practice

- Model sounding out the following word, saying each of the sounds quickly and clearly. Then blend the sounds together.

  c/r/ow/n   **crown**

- Now ask your child to sound out the word **crown**, showing a finger to represent each letter sound. (c/r/ow/n)
- Now ask your child to sound out and blend the following words. For each of the words, ask them to show a finger for each letter sound.

  cloak   flowers   brown

Extending vocabulary

- Look at pages 2 and 4 together and look for all the words that relate to trees. (e.g. *shoots, trunks, crowns, bark*)
- Now ask your child if they can tell you an antonym (opposite) for each of the following words:

highest	*(lowest)*	short	*(tall)*
bottom	*(top)*	little	*(big)*